KU-596-299

Getting Started

I have always been a daydreamer. Thoughts of history and art blend together in my mind, helping me create a whimsical world of carvings. Whether you are new to carving or an old pro, the projects and patterns you'll find here will give you hours of carving enjoyment. I hope you have as much fun carving these projects as I had creating them. May we meet down the road sometime and sit down and carve.

Thank you for visiting my world!

—Floyd Rhadigan

Here are a handful of the tools I use when carving my fantasy creatures. You can use the ones listed on the next page to carve your own projects, or you can select other tools that best suit you.

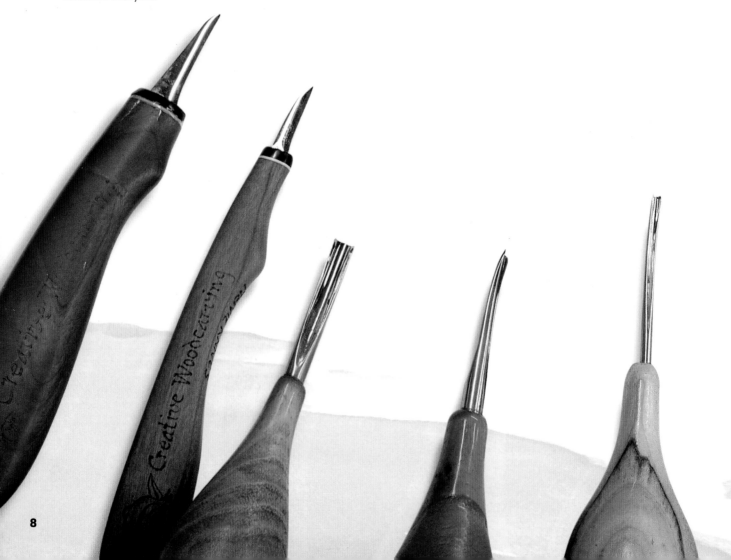

CARVING FANTASY
CREATURES

PATTERNS AND TECHNIQUES FOR 5 PROJECTS

Floyd Rhadigan

FOX CHAPEL
PUBLISHING

© 2012 by Floyd Rhadigan and Fox Chapel Publishing Company, Inc., East Petersburg, PA.

Carving Fantasy Creatures is an original work, first published in 2012 by Fox Chapel Publishing Company, Inc. The patterns contained herein are copyrighted by the author. Readers may make copies of these patterns for personal use. The patterns themselves, however, are not to be duplicated for resale or distribution under any circumstances. Any such copying is a violation of copyright law.

ISBN 978-1-56523-609-7

To learn more about the other great books from Fox Chapel Publishing, or to find a retailer near you, call toll-free 800-457-9112 or visit us at *www.FoxChapelPublishing.com*.

Note to Authors: We are always looking for talented authors to write new books. Please send a brief letter describing your idea to Acquisition Editor, 1970 Broad Street, East Petersburg, PA 17520.

Printed in Indonesia

First printing

About the Author

Floyd Rhadigan was introduced to woodcarving by a family friend in 1970 and immediately took to it, carving as many projects as he could and eventually buying his first carving book in 1973. Due to a shortage of carving tools on the market, Rhadigan primarily completed his projects using a carving knife, until a book by Harold Enlow introduced him to palm tools. As Rhadigan's skills grew, he began developing his own carving style, which he describes as a mix between Ozark and Flat Plane Scandinavian styles. Rhadigan began teaching his carving techniques in 1976 for the Mt. Clemens Adult Education Program in Mt. Clemens, Michigan. He has also taught carving classes for Warren Michigan's Parks and Recreation Department and in Saline, Michigan. Rhadigan now teaches regularly for the Creative Woodcarving Seminar (Cadillac, Michigan) and the Michigan Woodcarvers Association (Oscoda, Michigan). In addition he gives annual classes at the Wood Carvers Roundup (Evart, Michigan) and the Northeast Wood Carvers Roundup (Honesdale, Pennsylvania) and conducts seminars for individuals and carving clubs. To learn more, visit *www.fantasycarving.com*.

Author Floyd Rhadigan.

Contents

Basic Carving Instructions

I used a variety of palm tools to carve the projects in this booklet. Each project was made using the following tools:

- ½" (13mm) #9 gouge
- ½" (13mm) #7 gouge
- ½" (13mm) #3 gouge
- ¼" (6mm) #9 gouge
- ³⁄₁₆" (5mm) #9 gouge
- ⅛" (3mm) #9 gouge
- ¼" (6mm)-wide V-tool
- ³⁄₁₆" (5mm)-wide V-tool
- ⅛" (3mm)-wide V-tool
- 1¼" (32mm) bench knife
- ¾" (20mm) detail knife

You can use the tools I have listed or any other number of small gouges, V-tools, and knives you have on hand in your workshop and are comfortable using.

Keep your tools sharp by using a strop. You can also rub aluminum oxide stropping compound on a wood dowel or a length of wood shaped to the contour of your tools. By drawing the strop over the cutting edge, you can maintain sharp tools.

I prefer to use northern basswood for my carvings, because it carves well and will hold detail. All of the projects presented here were carved with the wood grain running up and down. To start carving your project, cut a wood blank to size and attach the front pattern. (If you'd like, you can purchase pre-cut blanks and rough outs from me by visiting *www.fantasycarving.com*, calling 734-649-3259, or by emailing me at *rhads134@comcast.net*.)

Cut the blank with a band saw, following the pattern. When I do this step, I leave a small tab of wood on the front of the cutout to help level the blank on the saw bed while I move on to cutting out the side view. Once you've cut out the front view, attach the side view pattern to your blank and cut it out with the saw.

Using the pictures of the project and pattern as a visual guide, start removing the excess wood from blank. Take your time; it is much easier to carve your piece to shape first and then carve in the details. Refer to your picture and pattern often.

I highly recommend wearing a Kevlar carving glove while you work. It is also important to keep your tools sharp. Sharp tools are actually much safer to work with than dull tools. Remember to take your time. Hasty work can result in a mistake on your carving or an accident with one of your tools.

Painting and Finishing

When your carving is all finished, make sure to sand away any remaining saw marks or other marks left on the wood as they accept paint and finish differently than carved areas. If left unsanded, these marks will be visible on the finished carving. Using a small scrub brush or denture brush, wash your carving with warm water and dish soap. Rinse it and let it dry.

Once your carving has dried, spray it with two light coats of a matte finish (I use Krylon #1311 Matte Finish). The finish will keep your paints from bleeding into each other as you work on your project. Always paint on your light colors first, and paint all background areas before adding the details.

Paint your projects using your preferred brand of acrylic paint. I use Jo Sonja and Delta Ceramcoat acrylic paints.

I prefer to thin the paint for my background colors, mixing twenty drops of water into every drop of paint. Diluting the paint this way allows the wood grain to show through the paint when the project is finished. For areas like the eyes, buttons, buckles, and other accessories like knives and swords, I don't thin the paint as much, allowing the color of these objects to stand out. If there is a specific part of your carving that you'd like to emphasize with color, paint it with a color you have only thinned a little bit. I also like to add flair to my carvings' clothing by adding pin stripes or a plaid pattern.

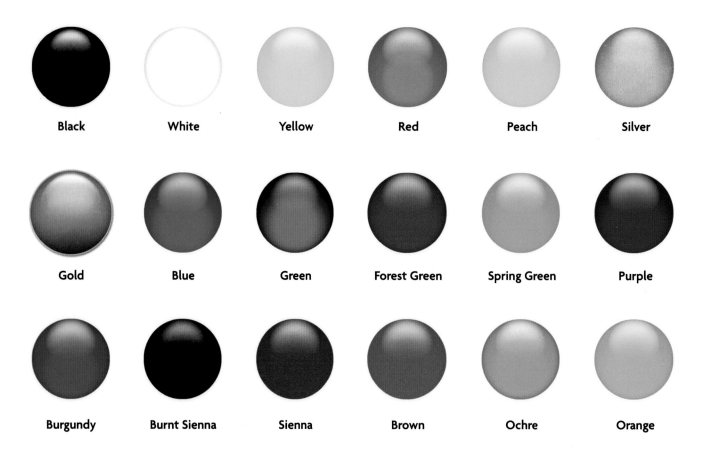

Color chart. These are some of the various colors I use for my carvings. I choose to use Jo Sonja and Delta Ceramcoat acrylic paints, but you can use your preferred brand of acrylic paint and vary the color choices as you desire.

Painting the eyes

I think the eyes bring life to any carving. The steps below demonstrate the method I use to paint eyes on my carvings and bring them to life. Before you start, cover the entire eye and eyelid area of your carving with a layer of flesh-colored paint and let dry.

Once you have finished painting, spray on one more coat of matte finish. Then, use a finishing wax to antique your carving. I use Watco Satin Finish Wax, making a mixture of about 70 percent natural wax and 30 percent dark wax. Use a small, stiff bristled brush to apply the wax to the entire carving. Pat it dry with a paper towel or rag to remove any excess, and then buff the carving.

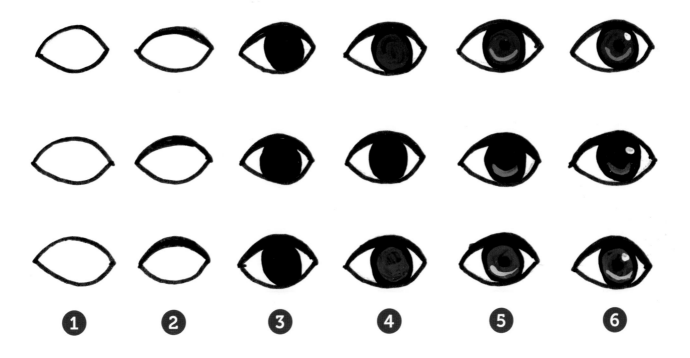

Painting Steps

1. Thin white paint just a bit and paint the eyeball, trying not to hit the lids. Let the paint dry*.

2. Use black to paint along the edge of the upper eyelid to thicken the lid.

3. Paint on the iris using black paint. I prefer to put the iris closer to the inner or outer corner of the eye. I find that placing the iris directly in the middle of the eye gives the carving a straight, blank stare. Let the paint dry.

4. Paint the iris color (blue, brown, or green) inside the black iris circle you painted during Step 3. Paint the colored circle small enough that a black ring surrounds the colored paint when you are finished.

5. Paint a small crescent on the lower part of the iris, using light blue on blues eyes, orange on brown eyes, and light green on green eyes. Then, use black to paint the pupil in the center of the iris.

6. Paint a speck of white on one side of the upper iris.

Note that you can use a hair dryer to help dry the paint and speed this process along.

Watchful Dragon

Dragons are one of my favorite creatures to carve. This friendly little caricature dragon is fairly easy to carve and paint. Most carvers will be able to take him from a block of wood to a finished carving in a weekend. He makes a great gift and will be glad to perch on your bookshelf or computer monitor, keeping an eye on things while you are busy with your next project.

I usually rough out carving blanks on a band saw. When cutting the first profile, I leave tabs of wood in strategic locations to make cutting the second profile easier. For this dragon, I leave a tab of wood on the side of one of his horns. This tab gives me two points of contact on the saw table and the tab is easy to carve off later.

After cutting both profiles, sketch the details onto the blank. I use a variety of knives and gouges to carve the dragon, but the most important tool I use is a pencil. As soon as I carve off a line, I draw it back on.

The most important thing to concentrate on is controlled and planned cuts. I rely heavily on relief cuts. Make your stop cut first, and then make the relief cut up to the stop cut. When the cuts meet, the chips will pop out and give you a clean cut. I use a ³⁄₁₆" (5mm)-wide V-tool to carve the toes.

After you complete the carving, seal the wood with a light coat of Krylon matte finish. When the matte finish is dry, paint the dragon. You can use my color scheme or get creative and develop your own. Seal the painted carving with another light coat of Krylon matte finish.

To antique the carving, create a mixture of 70 percent Watco natural finishing wax and 30 percent Watco dark finishing wax. Brush the wax on and wipe it off with a paper towel. Allow the wax to dry and then buff it with a clean cloth.

MATERIALS:

- 3" x 4¾" x 5" (76 x 121 x 127mm) basswood blank
- Krylon matte finish
- Watco natural finishing wax
- Watco dark finishing wax
- Acrylic paints of choice (I use Moss Green, Hookers Green, Ivory, and Purple)

TOOLS:

- Carving knives and gouges of choice
- ³⁄₁₆"-wide V-tool
- Band saw
- Pencil

Special Sources: *Basswood rough outs of the Watchful Dragon are available for $15 plus $4 s&h. Contact Floyd Rhadigan at 734-649-3259 or visit www.fantasycarving.com.*

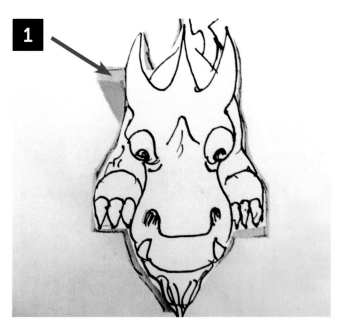

Leave a small tab next to the dragon's horns when cutting the front view. The tab keeps the blank level while you cut the side profile.

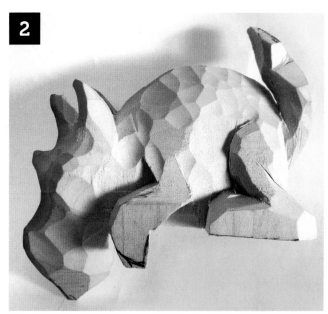

Carve the general shape of the dragon before adding the details.

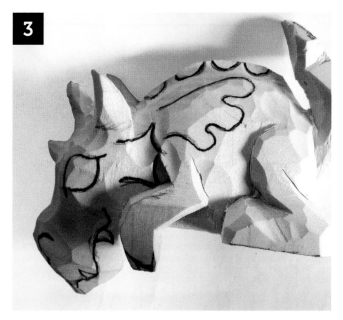

Repeatedly sketch in the pattern lines for a reference as you carve.

Clean up any rough cuts and make sure the dragon sits correctly before you begin painting.

Front

Left

Back

Right

Place your finished dragon on a shelf anywhere in your home to watch over you and your belongings.

The History of Dragons

Dragons have had a presence in cultures around the world from ancient times to the present. They appear on countless artifacts discovered by archaeologists and historians on almost every continent and are described in a myriad of stories and legends. In fact, the word "dragon" appears more than thirty times in the King James version of the Bible. Although science indicates dinosaurs and humans did not exist on the earth at the same time, it has been suggested that dragon legends and tales are accounts of human encounters with dinosaurs. If this were the case, it could explain why so many cultures placed great honor on men like St. George who could slay these terrifying creatures.

Not every culture recognizes dragons as creatures of evil. Most Eastern cultures hold a deep respect for the wisdom, intelligence, magic, and beauty of dragons. In Western cultures, however, dragons are most often depicted as monsters. This explains why dragons are included in Eastern celebrations and appear as a part of the Chinese calendar, while the West abounds with tales of ravenous creatures that threaten humanity.

The anatomy of dragons is widely varied and often differs from culture to culture. Some are depicted as having wings and the ability to breathe fire, others are serpent-like creatures that live in water, and still others have barbed tails and sharp claws.

Watchful Dragon

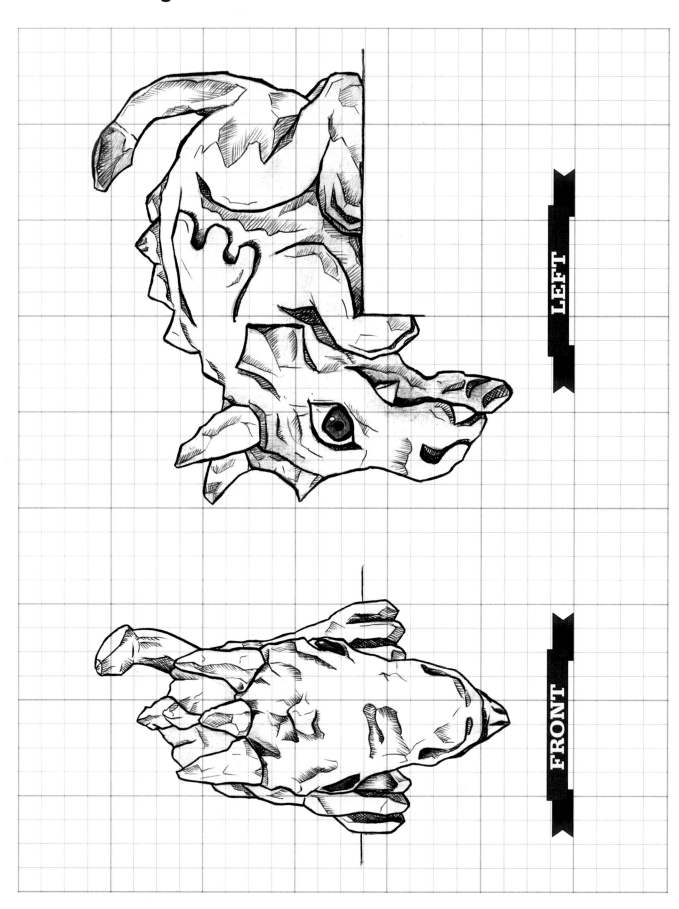

LEFT

FRONT

Watchful Dragon

RIGHT

BACK

Penelope Pig

With her hat and her purse, Penelope looks smart on her way to market. I like giving my animal carvings human characteristics; it gives the finished piece a caricature feel. Remember with this carving that pigs naturally have small eyes, so don't make Penelope's eyes too large.

Materials:

- A blank cut to 5" (127mm) high, 2½" (64mm) wide, and 2" (51mm) deep
- Krylon matte finish
- Watco natural finishing wax
- Watco dark finishing wax
- Acrylic paints of choice (I use Black, White, Flesh, Green, Yellow Ochre, Orange, and Burnt Sienna by Jo Sonja and Delta Ceramcoat)

Tools:

- Carving knives, gouges, and V-tools of choice
- Band saw
- Pencil

Special Sources: *Basswood rough outs of Penelope Pig are available for $12 plus s&h. Contact Floyd Rhadigan at 734-649-3259 or visit www.fantasycarving.com.*

The author used these products for the project. Substitute your choice of brands, tools, and materials as desired.

Front

Left

Back

Freyr and the Golden Boar

Freyr and his twin sister, Freyja, are gods of Norse mythology—Freyr, the god of fertility and prosperity, and Freyja, the goddess of love and fertility. As a god, Freyr had many powerful objects at his disposal, including a horse that, in some legends, could withstand fire and, in others, understood speech. He also had a ship large enough to hold an army of gods, but able to be folded up and placed in his pocket when not in use. According to legend, the ship would always sail where directed no matter the wind direction, or would always receive favorable winds. Freyr's weapon was a sword that would fight opponents on its own.

In addition, dwarves gave Freyr a golden boar. The boar was a very powerful animal that could travel over land, through the sky, and over water. It was said to be capable of outrunning any animal, and its golden bristles enabled Freyr to see it in the darkest places. Freyr could choose to ride the boar or have it pull his chariot. Many images of this god depict him riding or accompanied by this golden boar.

Right

Penelope Pig

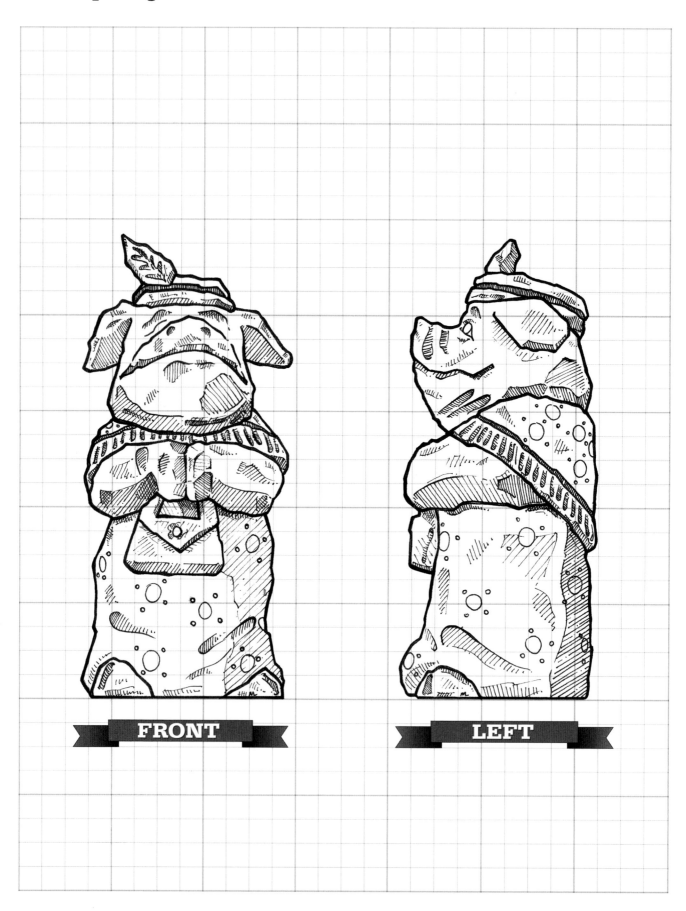

FRONT

LEFT

BACK

RIGHT

The Gargoyle

This carving doubles as a candleholder to light your castle. It is much easier to drill the hole for the candle before you carve the gargoyle. Before you start carving, drill a hole ¾" (19mm) wide and 1½" (38mm) deep in the top of the project. A Forstner bit does a great job, especially when used in a drill press.

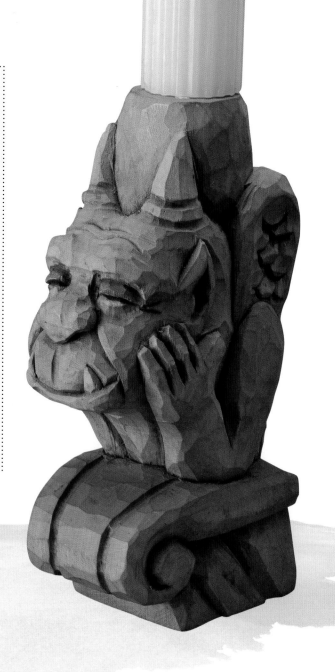

Materials:

- A blank cut to 6½" (165mm) high, 2½" (64mm) wide, and 3¼" (83mm) deep
- Krylon matte finish
- Watco natural finishing wax
- Watco dark finishing wax
- Acrylic paints of choice (I use Grey, Moss Green, White, Burnt Sienna, and Black by Jo Sonja and Delta Ceramcoat)

Tools:

- Carving knives, gouges, and V-tools of choice
- Band saw
- Pencil

Special Sources: *Basswood rough outs of the Gargoyle are available for $18 plus s&h. Contact Floyd Rhadigan at 734-649-3259 or visit www.fantasycarving.com.*

The author used these products for the project. Substitute your choice of brands, tools, and materials as desired.

Front

Left

Back

Right

Top

The Truth About Gargoyles

While most typically associated with cathedrals and castles throughout Europe, gargoyles and similar structures have been discovered in ancient Egyptian, Sumerian, Babylonian, Greek, and Roman ruins. Although many use the term "gargoyle" to refer to any creature-like statue or adornment on a building, true gargoyles are designed as rainspouts or gutters to keep rainwater from eroding the walls of the structures on which they are perched. In most cases, water leaves the gargoyle through its mouth. This explains the Latin root word for gargoyle, *gargula*, which means "gullet" or "throat." Other decorative elements incorporated into the architectural design of a building but that do not serve as rainspouts are called grotesques, while statues placed at building entrances are called guardians.

Gargoyles frequently take the shape of animals, some of the most popular being monkeys, pigs, lions, birds, goats, and dogs. In medieval times, the animal carved often had a specific meaning, like an association with evil or loyalty. Many gargoyles take the form of chimeras: creatures made up of parts from various animals, like a sphinx or a gryphon.

There are many theories explaining why the people of Europe and other areas chose to adorn their rain gutters with such fantastic carvings. Some suggest gargoyles represented demons and served as reminders of hell for medieval parishioners entering a cathedral. On the other end of the spectrum, some believe gargoyles served as protectors, carved with frightening features to scare away demons. It's also possible gargoyles represented condemned souls or were carved for reasons of pure entertainment.

Gargoyles, grotesques, and guardians can be found on structures throughout the world. The cathedral of Notre Dame in Paris is renowned for its veritable army of gargoyles, while China's Forbidden City is home to some of the most well-known guardian structures. Modern gargoyles can be seen on the National Cathedral in Washington, D.C.

The Gargoyle

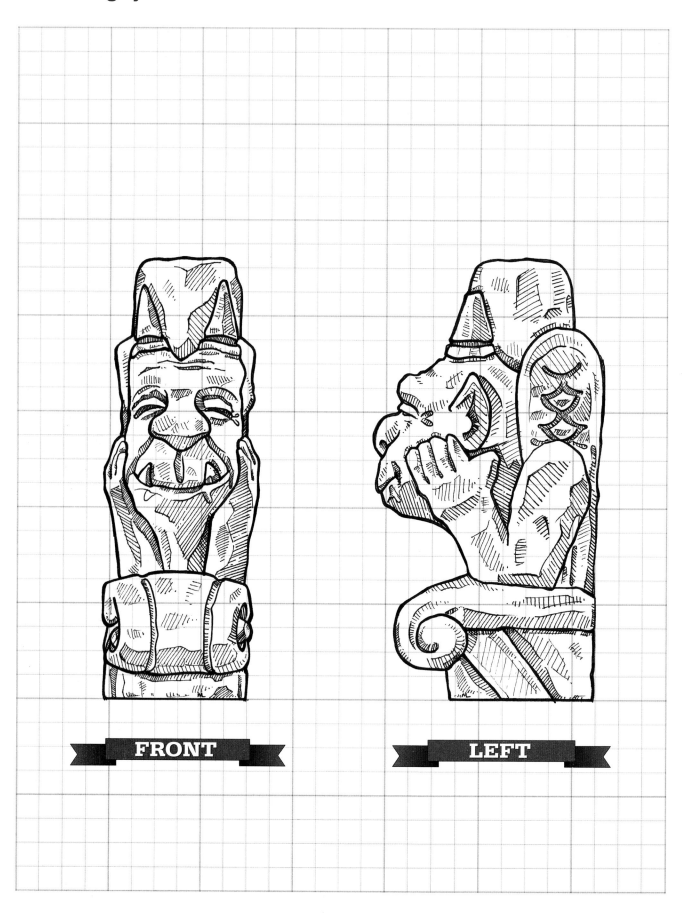

FRONT

LEFT

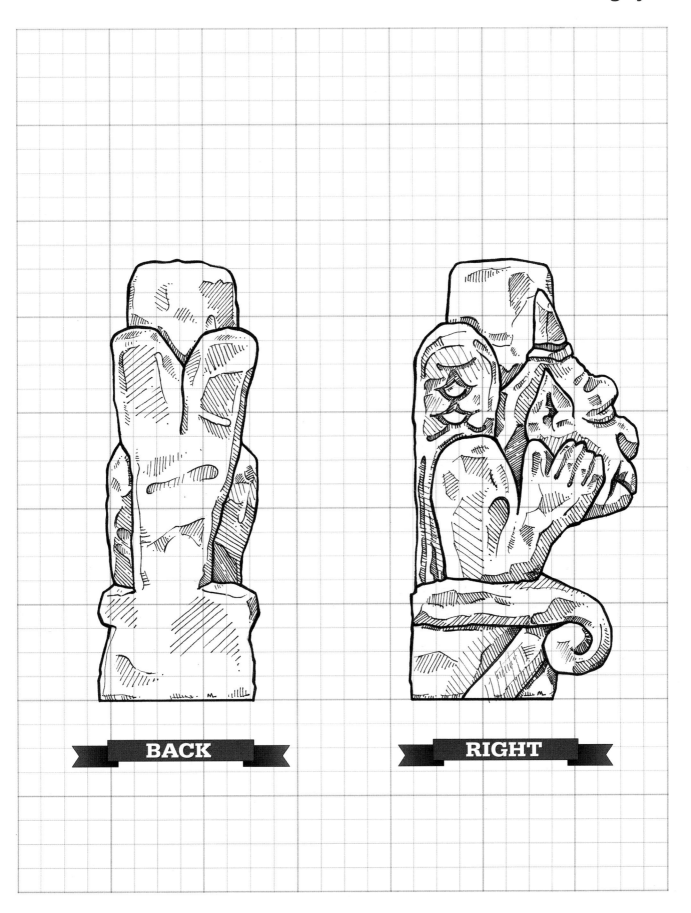

BACK

RIGHT

Alien Aquatic

This guy may be from another planet, but don't worry, he's a friendly sort. To make placing the trident insert easier, drill a ³⁄₁₆" (5mm) hole in the wood before carving the hand. Then, shape the hand and carve the trident to fit the hole.

Materials:

- A blank cut to 7" (178mm) high, 3" (76mm) wide, and 3" (76mm) deep
- Krylon matte finish
- Watco natural finishing wax
- Watco dark finishing wax
- Acrylic paints of choice (I use Black, White, Yellow, Moss Green, and Gold by Jo Sonja and Delta Ceramcoat)

Tools:

- Carving knives, gouges, and V-tools of choice
- Band saw
- Pencil

Special Sources: *Basswood rough outs of Alien Aquatic are available for $18 plus s&h. Contact Floyd Rhadigan at 734-649-3259 or visit www.fantasycarving.com.*

The author used these products for the project. Substitute your choice of brands, tools, and materials as desired.

Front

Left

Back

Area 51

Area 51 is a military base located in Nevada in the area surrounding Groom Lake that has been used for decades as a nuclear testing site and for aircraft development. Under the direction of organizations like the CIA and the United States Air Force, the base has been used to study Soviet aircraft and develop reconnaissance and stealth aircraft considered essential to national security. Because of the top secret nature of the projects and aircraft being developed in Area 51, the military base is under heavy security, including a no-fly zone that surrounds the base and extends vertically all the way to space.

The fact that little is known about Area 51 or the activities that take place there and that it is heavily guarded have sparked a great deal of curiosity about the base, along with a number of conspiracy theories. Many sightings of lights in the sky or strange flying objects have been reported in connection with the area, quickly developing into theories about alien technology being tested by the government. This controversy was furthered by the reports of Robert Lazar, who claimed to have worked in Area 51 and have knowledge of alien technology on the base. Most recognize the reported lights and flying objects are likely the results of standard aircraft development and testing. Some have claimed the conspiracy theories surrounding Area 51 have actually helped keep secret the many national defense projects underway at the base.

Right

Alien Aquatic

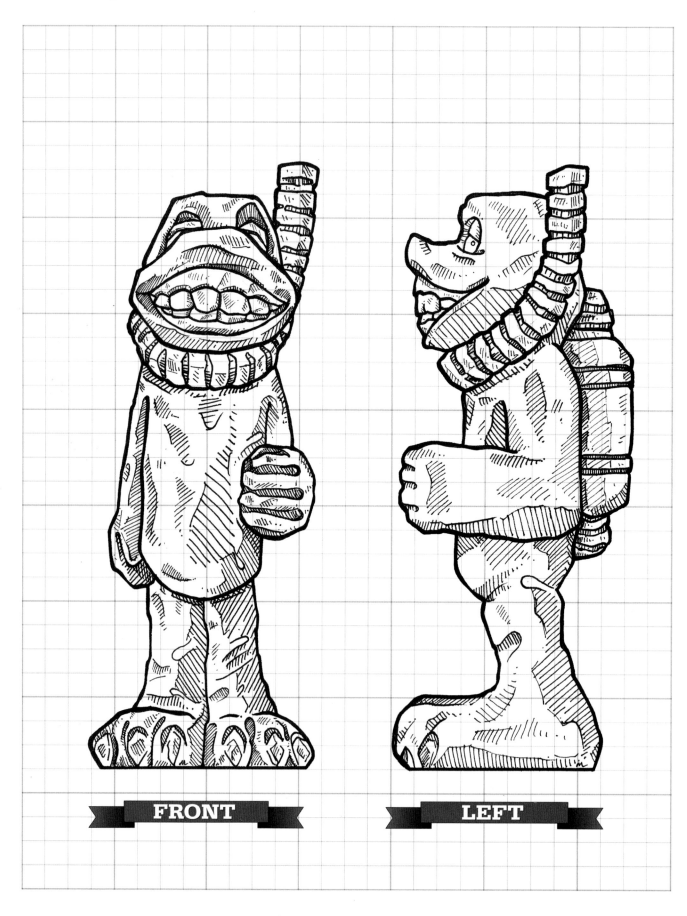

FRONT

LEFT

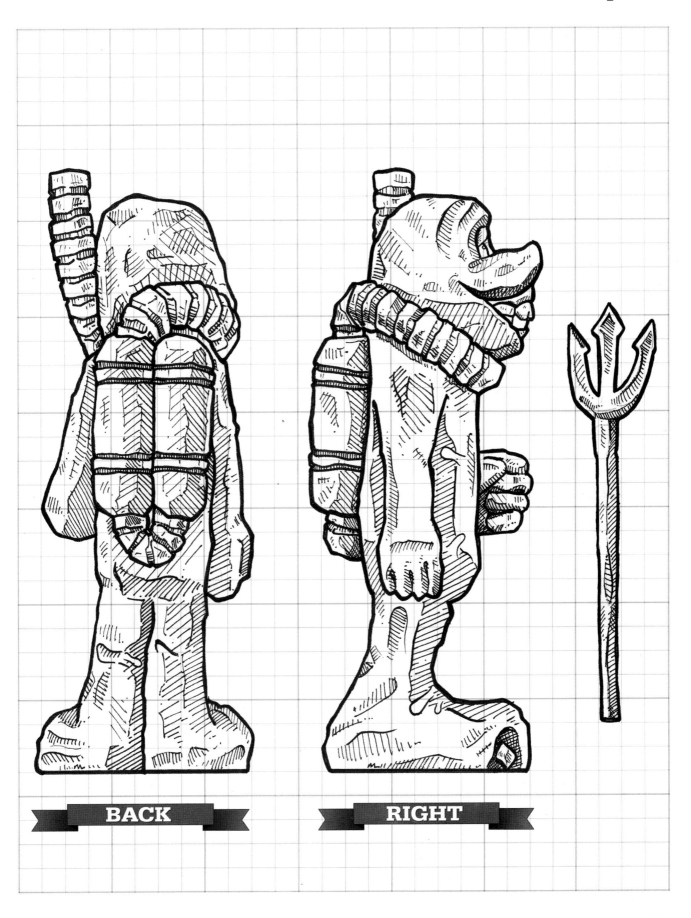

BACK

RIGHT

Reptilian Knight

He is a gruesome figure, ready to fight with his spear and saber. Drill the ³⁄₁₆" (5mm) hole for the spear before you carve the knight's left hand. Then, shape the hand and carve the spear to fit the hole. You'll want to carve the horns on his helmet last.

Materials:

- A blank cut to 7¾" (197mm) high, 3¾" (95mm) wide, and 3" (76mm) deep
- Krylon matte finish
- Watco natural finishing wax
- Watco dark finishing wax
- Acrylic paints of choice (I use Black, Silver, Burgundy, Burnt Umber, Gold, Moss Green, and Yellow by Jo Sonja and Delta Ceramcoat)

Tools:

- Carving knives, gouges, and V-tools of choice
- Band saw
- Pencil

Special Sources: *Basswood rough outs of the Reptilian Knight are available for $20 plus s&h. Contact Floyd Rhadigan at 734-649-3259 or visit www.fantasycarving.com.*

The author used these products for the project. Substitute your choice of brands, tools, and materials as desired.

Front

Left

Back

The Basilisk

According to mythology, the basilisk is an incredibly powerful reptile, often referred to as the "king" of serpents. Some legends hold that it is a cross between a rooster and a snake. One of the earliest descriptions of a basilisk comes from Pliny the Elder. Contrary to other depictions of the basilisk as a large and powerful beast, Pliny writes of the creature as a small snake, not much longer than the span of two hands. Despite its small size, Pliny's basilisk has incredibly powerful venom and is capable of killing any who meet its gaze. The basilisk seems to have a slightly different appearance than a serpent, moving about with the front portion of its body held erect. Some images of the creature have a strong resemblance to a dragon, and it is often depicted with wings.

Although incredibly deadly, a basilisk could be killed in a number of ways. A rooster's crow was said to be deadly to the basilisk. Dropping a weasel into its den could also destroy the creature (this legend is perhaps connected to the natural relationship between the cobra and the mongoose). Finally, a basilisk's power could be turned on itself by holding a mirror up to its face, causing it to meet its own gaze.

Right

Reptilian Knight

FRONT

LEFT

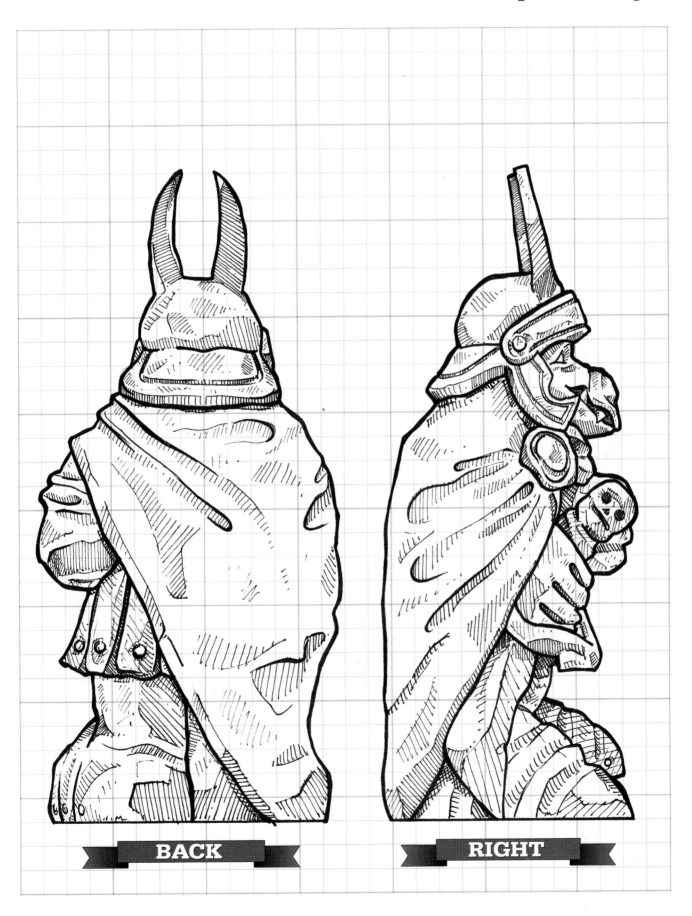

BACK

RIGHT

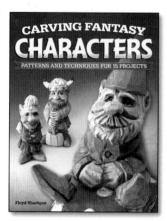

Carving Fantasy Characters
ISBN: 978-1-56523-749-0 **$16.99**

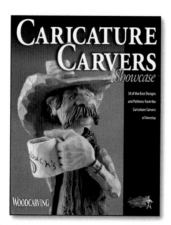

Caricature Carvers Showcase
ISBN: 978-1-56523-337-9 **$19.95**

Whittling Little Folk
ISBN: 978-1-56523-518-2 **$16.95**

Big Book of Whittle Fun
ISBN: 978-1-56523-520-5 **$12.95**

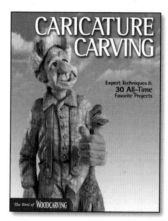

Caricature Carving (Best of WCI)
ISBN: 978-1-56523-474-1 **$19.95**

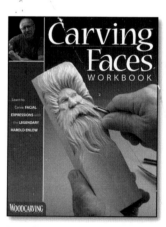

Carving Faces Workbook
ISBN: 978-1-56523-585-4 **$19.95**

WOODCARVING
ILLUSTRATED

In addition to being a leading source of woodworking books and DVDs, Fox Chapel also publishes *Woodcarving Illustrated*. Released quarterly, it delivers premium projects, expert tips and techniques from today's finest carvers, and in-depth information about the latest tools, equipment, and materials.

Subscribe Today!
Woodcarving Illustrated: **888-506-6630**
www.FoxChapelPublishing.com